MIGHTY MACHINES

MIGHTY MACHINES

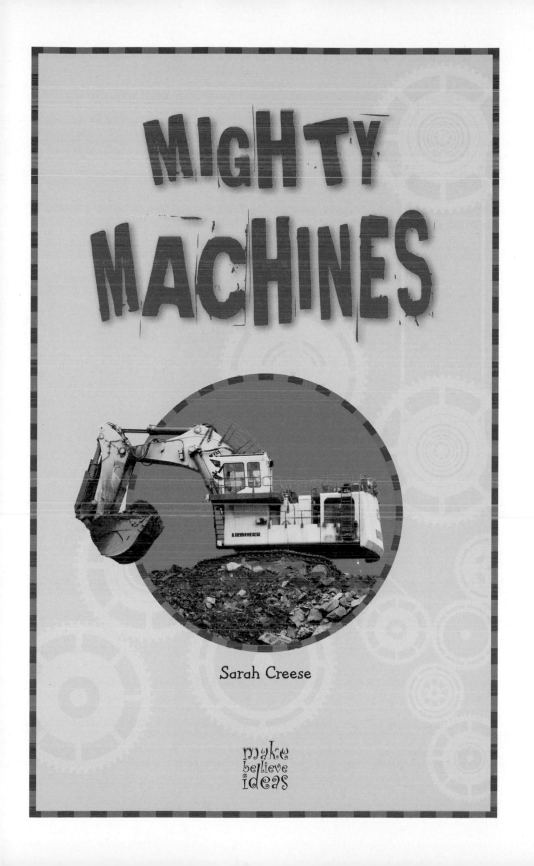

Sarah Creese

make
believe
ideas

Mighty machines can do it all.
There's no job too heavy, big, or small!
With big wheels and buckets,
they're strong and tough.
They can work when it's raining,
muddy, or rough.

Copyright © 2010 make believe ideas ltd.
27 Castle Street, Berkhamsted, Hertfordshire, HP4 2DW.

Reading together

This book is an ideal first reader for your child, combining simple words and sentences with stunning color photography of vehicles.

Here are some of the many ways you can help your child take those first steps in reading. Encourage your child to:

- Look at and explore the detail in the pictures.
- Sound out the letters in each word.
- Read and repeat each short sentence.

Look at the pictures

Make the most of each page by talking about the pictures and finding key words. Here are some questions you can use to discuss each page as you go along:

- Why do you like this machine?
- What job does it do?
- What color is it?
- What kind of wheels does it have?

Look at rhymes

Some of the sentences in this book are simple rhymes. Encourage your child to recognize rhyming words. Try asking the following questions:

- What does this word say?
- Can you find a word that rhymes with it?

- Look at the ending of two words that rhyme. Are they spelled the same? For example, "truck" and "stuck," and "sky" and "high."

Test understanding

It is one thing to understand the meaning of individual words, but you need to make sure that your child understands the facts in the text.

- Play "find the obvious mistake." Read the text as your child looks at the words with you, but make an obvious mistake to see if he or she catches it. Ask your child to correct you and provide the right word.
- After reading the facts, close the book and think up questions to ask your child.
- Ask your child whether a fact is true or false.
- Provide your child with three answers to a question and ask him or her to pick the correct one.

Quiz pages

At the end of the book there is a simple quiz. Ask the questions and see if your child can remember the right answers from the text. If not, encourage him or her to look up the answers.

Mighty machines

With massive wheels and big buckets, these mighty machines can lift, load, dig, and dump. They help us with tough jobs all over the world!

Load me up;
I'm a giant dump truck.
I can move through mud,
and I'll never get stuck!

mirror

driver's cab

grille

wheel

I have lots of wheels.
Can you count each one?
I can move the biggest loads.
I'll get the job done!

bucket

tracks

I am an excavator.
I am strong and big.
My tracks help me to move,
and my bucket helps me dig!

Wheel loader

bucket

tire chains

I'm a mighty wheel loader;
put me to the test!
I move earth with my bucket;
it's the biggest and the best!

driver's cab

wheel

boom

driver's cab

I'm a mighty crane.
I stretch down from the sky.
I use my long boom
to lift loads way up high.

wheel

I'm a giant tractor.
I can pull and I can haul;
heavy plows or big drills—
I can pull them all!

I'm a demolition machine.
I crush and bash.
I can break down buildings—
watch out for the crash!

I am a big rig.
I drive all day and night.
My trailer carries
heavy loads.
I'm definitely
not light!

OVERSIZE LOAD

T3 - 120

Look at my tires!
They're giant, tall, and fat.

I drive over cars
and crush them flat!

I turn and dig to make holes in the ground.

I'm a bucket wheel excavator: the largest machine around!

What do

1. Which mighty machine can break down buildings?

A demolition excavator.

2. How does a giant excavator move?

A giant excavator moves using its tracks.

3. Which mighty machine carries loads all day and night?

A big rig.

you know?

4. What can a giant tractor pull?

A giant tractor can pull plows and drills.

5. What type of tires does a monster truck have?

A monster truck has giant, tall, and fat tires.

6. Which mighty machine can lift loads very high?

A mobile crane.

Dictionary

machine

A machine is something with lots of parts that work together to do a job.

driver's cab

The driver's cab is the place where the driver sits in a truck, loader, or a digger.

load

Trucks carry loads. A load is usually heavy and large.

boom

A boom is a long, metal arm found on machines.

haul

Tractors haul things by pulling or dragging them.